THE ROTTINGDEAN YEARS

For Mrs Elizabeth Dacre M.B.E., T.D., J.P.
who loves Rottingdean
and has done so much for the village
over so many years

I am particularly indebted to Lady Mansergh
and her daughter Mrs Hilary Webber
for permitting me to quote from letters sent to them
by their family friend, Rudyard Kipling

I am also most grateful to
Mr E. H. Marsh, and Mr. J. G. Davies
for reading the script and making
very helpful comments.

MICHAEL SMITH has written a number of books on geological and geographical themes and now, in retirement from teacher education, lectures in a part-time capacity for the Centre for Continuing Education of the University of Sussex. He specialises on topics relating to the landscapes, the historical geography and literary heritage of the county.

ISBN 0 9515107 0 3

CONTENTS

ILLUSTRATIONS

I am indebted to the National Portrait Gallery for permission to reproduce Plate 3 and to the Rottingdean Preservation Society for plates 1, 5 & 6.

THE ROTTINGDEAN YEARS

Rottingdean recalls, with justifiable pride, the period of Rudyard Kipling's residence in the village between 1897 and 1902. He and his family were, however, inveterate travellers and much of each winter was spent away, so membership of the village community was not continuous. Those years were notable for joy as well as sadness, for peace as well as conflict, but above all for the exceptional quality of the work he produced within the comfortable ambience of his extended family living in the little valley running to the sea.

Rudyard Kipling's initial visit to Rottingdean came when he was 'en route' to rejoin his parents in India in 1882. He had just left the United Services College at Westward Ho!, near Bideford, and was to take up an appointment as Assistant Editor on the 'Civil and Military Gazette' in Lahore where his father was Curator of the Museum. He had suffered, as a child, both from the separation from his parents and at the hands of an apparently cruel landlady and her equally unpleasant son in lodgings in Southsea. He had been placed under her care, a common practice for children of the Empire, at the age of six, in 1871. He remained with the Holloway family until he went to the school, founded only four years earlier, designed to prepare boys of expatriate parents for a career in imperial enterprise. His years at Lorne Lodge in Southsea, his 'forlorn lodge', or the 'House of Desolation', were relieved only by occasional holidays in Fulham with his 'beloved Aunt', Georgiana Burne-Jones, who, by 1882 had a holiday home in one of the 'Green Properties', 'Prospect House', in the village. He spent just a few days with her family before embarking, not yet seventeen years of age, for the India where he was to make so dramatic a literary impact.

Certainly he cut his teeth, journalistically, first on the 'C & M' in Lahore and then on its senior partner 'The Pioneer' in Allahabad. For both, in addition to the normal run of the mill reporting and editing, he was able to publish short stories and poems drawing upon his acute observation not only of the foibles of those working on behalf of the Raj on the plains and relaxing in the hill-stations, but also in the less salubrious milieu of city back streets, bazaars and caravanserais. The poems were collected and published as *Departmental Ditties* and *Barrack Room Ballads* whilst the prose became *Plain Tales from the Hills* and stories for the Indian Railway Library. Thus by 1889, on his return via North America, after his Indian experience was complete, he was already something of a literary lion. It was not, however, until after further travels and a period living in his wife Caroline's hometown of Brattleboro in Vermont that he was ready to settle in England. Even then the word 'settle' is overstating the case for he was, for many years, to spend a sizeable portion of each English winter in a warmer climate.

In September 1896 the Kipling family, for there were now Josephine and Elsie to delight their parents, lighted upon Maidencombe, near Torquay where they leased 'Rock House'. The choice of Devon was, perhaps, because he wished to share the nostalgia for the countryside he had first enjoyed whilst at school, and which was shortly to feature in print in *Stalky and Co.* Whilst they were there Kipling was invited to visit The Royal Naval College at Dartmouth, and accepting the chance of sea experience, was to begin a long, fruitful and happy liaison with the Senior Service.

Devon soon proved not to be the haven anticipated and so in the spring of the following year they fled to London pleading a broken cistern as the reason for their departure. In June they arrived to stay with Aunt Georgie at her holiday home in Rottingdean. She and her husband Edward had added the adjoining property 'Aubrey Cottage' to their original 'Prospect House' and had renamed them 'North End House' partly because it was appropriately near to the northern boundary of the village but also because their house in Fulham was in North End Road. Kipling in his autobiography, published at the end of his life and called *Something of Myself* describes the scene quite beautifully.

North End House.

The three properties are quite distinct. 'Prospect House' is on the left, 'Aubrey Cottage' in the middle and 'Gothic House' on the right. The first two were joined by Edward Burne-Jones as 'North End House'. The garden wall of 'The Elms' borders the criss-cross of the village green.

Our flight from Torquay ended almost by instinct at Rottingdean where beloved Aunt and Uncle had their holiday house, and where I had spent the last few days before sailing to India fourteen years back. In 1882 there had been but one daily bus from Brighton, which took forty minutes; and when a stranger appeared on the village green the native young would stick out their tongues at him. The Downs poured almost direct into the one village street and lay out eastward unbroken to Russia Hill above Newhaven. It was little altered in '96. My cousin, Stanley Baldwin, had married the eldest daughter of the Ridsdales out of the Dene – the big house that flanked one side of the green. My Uncle's 'North End House' commanded the other, and a third house opposite the church was waiting to be taken according to the decrees of Fate. The Baldwin marriage, then, made us free of the joyous young brotherhood and sisterhood of the Dene, and its friends. The Aunt and Uncle had said to us; "Let the child that is coming to you be born in our house", and effaced themselves till my son John arrived on a warm August night of '97, under what seemed every good omen. Meantime we had rented by direct interposition of Fate that third house opposite the church on the green. It stood in a sort of a little island behind flint walls which we then thought were high enough, and almost beneath some big ilex trees. It was small, none too well built, but cheap, and so suited us who remembered a little affair at Yokohama. Then there grew up great happiness between 'The Dene', 'North End House' and 'The Elms'. One could throw a cricket ball from any one house to the other, but beyond turning out at 2 A.M. to help a silly foxhound puppy who had stuck in a drain, I do not remember any alarms and excursions other than packing farm carts filled with mixed babies – Stanley Baldwin's and ours – and despatching them into the safe clean heart of the motherly Downs for jam-smeared picnics. Those Downs moved me to write some verses called 'Sussex'.

'The Elms' in Kipling's time. The ivy-clad garden wall and more trees than at present provided a certain seclusion.

The Kiplings leased 'The Elms', recently inherited by a Mr A.H.A. Bliss, attractively advertised as a 'marine Residence' for three guineas a week. Later on Kipling approached the owner with a view to purchase. The quoted price drew the response "Obviously you think there is a goldmine under the green at Rottingdean." The comment *none too well built, but cheap* was substantiated by the account during the writing of *Kim*, *the sou'-wester raged day and night, till the silly windows jiggled their wedges loose. (Which was why the Committee vowed never to have a house of their own with up-and-down windows.).* Perhaps it was these structural shortcomings which inspired the humourous *The Architect's Alphabet* recently rediscovered by Kenneth Baker in the Archive at the University of Sussex when he was preparing his anthology of English History in Verse. The 'Ambo' in the last line of *The Alphabet* referred to his cousin Ambrose Poynter who was an architect of modest ability and at whose hand his cousin seems to have suffered. The fact that 'The Elms' could be leased cheaply, *and so suited us who still remembered a little affair at Yokohama* was on account of his loss of capital by the unexpected collapse of the local branch of his Bank whilst in Japan.

Although the family began the move before John's birth on August 17th 1897, Carrie remained with Aunt Georgie throughout her confinement. The reference to his relations who formed a distinctive little colony in the village is fascinating, springing as it did from the marriages made by his mother's sisters. Kipling's mother Alice was one of the Macdonald girls, four of whom married remarkable men and produced some equally talented children. Georgiana – 'Georgie' – married Edward Burne-Jones, the artist and one of the Pre-Raphaelite brotherhood, later knighted. Agnes the third sister 'Aggie' had married Edward Poynter, another artist, later also knighted and President of the Royal Academy, whilst the fourth sister, Louisa, 'Louie' in Victorian diminutive, had married the wealthy ironmaster Alfred Baldwin. It was their son, Stanley, a future Prime Minister and the First Earl Baldwin, who had married Lucy, daughter of Edward L.J. Ridsdale of 'The Dene', the acknowledged Squire of the village. A fifth sister Edith was the only surviving one to remain unmarried. Assorted members of the extended family would gather in the village at various times, with their friends most of whom were equally interesting. Georgie, his 'beloved Aunt' was, in residence at 'North End House' which until the 1920's, was confined to the linked 'Prospect House' and 'Aubrey Cottage'. 'Gothic House' was added to the Burne-Jones property by Sir Roderick Jones, no relation of the former owner, to extend it still further. It is 'Gothic House' which now bears the more nostalgic, but perhaps less apposite name of the triple properties above its portico.

The village, when the Kiplings arrived on Derby Day in Queen Victoria's Diamond Jubilee Year of 1897, was very compact by comparison with today's limits. Essentially it covered the High Street, running up from the cliffline, then rather further seaward than today and the terminus at the short pier for the newly opened Brighton and Rottingdean Seashore Electric Railway. The present car park abutting the coast road formed a triangular block of buildings opposite which 'The White Horse', formerly the 'King of Prussia' was modest when compared with the present hotel. On the cliff edge to the south of the coastal road was a substantial building long since lost to cliff recession. Apart from the 'Green properties' a few houses crept up Nevill Road from the little nucleus of the school on the wider patch just landward of 'The Black Horse'. Past the farms and barns north of 'The Elms' garden a few houses were scattered, most notably 'Northgate House', the home of Sir Edward Carson the Ulster politician and one, less pretentious, 'Shepherd's Cottage', once the home of John Dudeney. A preparatory school recently established, Rottingdean School, occupied the area now encompassed by the Rotyngs. So *the Downs poured almost direct into the one village street* was succinct and accurate. The Green itself, mainly between the pond and 'The Elms' was criss-crossed by a little network of tracks.

Circumstances combined to make the Rottingdean years particularly fruitful and some of his finest work, both prose and poetry, was created or developed within the fold of the Downs. The distinctive rounded contours of the chalk hills inspired a deep and lasting admiration and even when he had moved to the contrasting landscape of the inner Weald, the Downland still called him. Indeed his little tribute to their crests, called *The Run of the Downs* written for *Rewards and Fairies* begins *The Weald is good, the Downs are best, I'll give you the run of 'em East to West*. But he understood not only the physical landscape created by nature but also the way in which the hand of man left still recognisable marks as much as six millenia later. His poem *Sussex* which *Those Downs moved me to write* encapsulates his quite extraordinary grasp of the essentials of the development of the natural and human landscape. He recognised the capacity of the chalk to absorb rain and thus to leave the dry-valleys without streams. How marvellously *Our blunt bow-headed, whale-backed Downs*, and *We have no waters to delight our broad and brookless vales* – capture their unique character. But his descriptive powers of this increasingly familiar, tranquil and time forgotten scene is even more vividly recreated in the opening of *The Knife and the Naked Chalk* which follows *The Run of the Downs.*

The children went to the seaside for a month, and lived in a flint village on the bare windy chalk Downs, quite thirty miles from home. They made friends with an old shepherd, called Mr. Dudeney, who had known their father when their father was little. *****

One August afternoon when the village water-cart had made the street smell specially townified, they went to look for their shepherd as usual, and as usual, Old Jim crawled over the door-step and took them in charge. The sun was hot, the dry grass was very slippery and the distances were very distant.

'It's just like the sea,' said Una, when Old Jim halted in the shade of a lonely flint barn on a bare rise. 'You see where you're going, and – you go there, and there's nothing between.' ******

The children went on. Two kestrels hung bivvering and squealing above them. A gull flapped lazily along the white edge of the cliffs. The curves of the Downs shook a little in the heat, and so did Mr. Dudeney's distant head.

They walked toward it very slowly and found themselves staring into a horse-shoe shaped hollow a hundred feet deep, whose steep sides were laced with tangled sheep-tracks. The flock grazed on the flat at the bottom, under the charge of Young Jim. Mr. Dudeney sat comfortably knitting on the edge of the slope, his crook between his knees. ****

The air trembled a little as though it could not make up its mind whether to slide into the Pit or move across the open. But it seemed easiest to go down-hill, and the children felt one soft puff after another slip and sidle down the slope in fragrant breaths that baffed on their eyelids. The little whisper of the sea by the cliffs joined with the whisper of the wind over the grass, the hum of the insects in the thyme, the ruffle and rustle of the flock below, and a thickish mutter deep in the very chalk beneath them.

By the time of *Puck of Pook's Hill* and *Rewards and Fairies* the family had moved to Bateman's, but here, the children Dan and Una, in reality his own John and Elsie, were the instruments by which Puck was able to introduce them to characters from British history. In *The Knife and the Naked Chalk* they meet a Stone-Age man who has to make a sacrifice in order to save his tribe, and the story is set in the Downland to the east of the village of Rottingdean. Kipling frequently plucked well known local names for use and that of Dudeney is one of very long standing in Rottingdean. The most remarkable of the Rottingdean shepherds was John Dudeney, the 'scholar shepherd' who supplemented his meagre salary by trapping moles and catching wheatears, the latter activity a traditional one locally. He used the extra income on buying books and his scholarship was tutored under the eye of the Vicar, the Reverend Dr. Hooker at the turn of the Eighteenth Century. Soon he was taken into the publishing business of Baxter's in Lewes and thence into schoolmastering. But it was Ben Dudeney, working the sheep around the village of Kipling's time, upon whom the character was almost certainly drawn. Another local name is used in the story *The Comprehension of Private Copper*, in *Traffics and Discoveries* and is drawn upon the long-established farming family, then great characters in the village and still active in the locality. Bob Copper is a folk singer of renown, an artist, poet and an award-winning chronicler of Rottingdean in *A Song for Every Season* and *Early to Rise*. But the name used more than any other, both in prose and poetry, was also familiar in Rottingdean in Kipling's day, although later he had a friend named Hobden in the Weald. The character of Hobden, the hedger, ditcher and poacher, and his Roman predecessor, Hobdenius, was, however, drawn on a Burwash man named Isted. Hobden stands, throughout the Puck stories, pre-eminently, for the timeless, stolid wisdom of the countryman.

Although Kipling spent the winter away he became very much part of the village scene, an object of awe because of his fame, but one treated not only with some deference but also with the half-mocking refusal of farmhands to take him with unqualified respect. His unusual christian name, given after Rudyard Lake a spot, near Leek in Staffordshire, dear to the heart of his parents during their courtship, was altered by the locals to 'Barnyard' as a term of humorous endearment. There are a few amusing anecdotes of his time as a 'Rottingdeaner'. R. Thurston Hopkins has recorded that although pleased to be recognised as a famous name he was not always keen to have his privacy encroached upon. It irked him that the driver of the horse-bus bringing trippers from Brighton would, if encountering him on a circuit of the village, point him out with his whip to passengers and declare in stentorian tones "Here we have Mr. Kiplin', the soldiers' poet." He contained himself until, one day, the driver, somewhat careless, damaged a sapling near the pond. He wrote a fierce letter of complaint to the landlord of 'The White Horse' who was also the proprietor of the horse-bus. The inn-keeper presented the letter to his cronies in the bar parlour and they advised calm indifference, advice which he took. One of the customers proffered 10/- for the autographed letter and this, too, was accepted. As Kipling received no reply he wrote a second and doubly vehement letter the following day. Perceiving a market the publican obtained £1 for the letter of twice the power. Still no response, so on the third day Kipling stormed into the inn to seek redress. The landlord's reaction was of devastating logical simplicity. "Why Sir, I was hoping you'd send me a fresh one every day, they pay a deal better than bus-driving." A slightly different version of the story is to be found in Lord Birkenhead's meticulous biography. In his account the complaint was made about the driver stopping by the gate of 'The Elms' and the landlord is said to have cut out the signature and stuck it in an autograph album. We shall never know which, if either, is true.

Kipling was also at loggerheads with the landlord of 'The Plough' for during the Boer War, Blaber was determinedly a 'Little Englander' who believed that the country should not be involved in imperial adventures. Kipling, with his first-hand knowledge of the war through his annual trips to South Africa, not only believed in the cause espoused by his friends Cecil Rhodes, Lord Milner and Dr. Starr Jameson, but supported it and worked actively to alleviate the suffering of the families of the soldiers. Their arguments were fierce and acrimonious until Blaber's doctor asked Kipling to desist, fearing that his patient would suffer a heart attack if the exchanges continued. His beloved Aunt Georgie did not share her nephew's view of the war either. On the announcement of the Treaty of Vereeniging bringing the war to an end in June 1902 she displayed a banner from the first floor bay window of 'North End House' bearing the legend "We have killed and also taken possession" a quotation from I Kings, Chapter 21, Verse 19. This incensed the locals, many of whom were involved in Kipling's patriotically inspired movements. An ugly incident might well have developed had not Kipling and his cousin, Ambrose Poynter, acted as peacemakers. Colonel Moens in his charming book *Rottingdean – The story of a village* ascribes this incident to the news of the Relief of Mafeking in May 1900, whereas all Kipling's major biographers give the later date. Kipling did celebrate the news from Mafeking by firing a cannon from the cliff and arranged improvised rattling of tin-cans to welcome the happy day. As on the later occasion Aunt Georgie together with her daughter Margaret and her son-in-law Jack Mackail were less than joyous, feeling that the war diminished Britain's standing as a civilized nation.

On his return from South Africa in the Spring of 1898 he began work on a story which was to become one of his most important and critically acclaimed books, *Kim*. He was able to do so because he found the congenial company of his Uncle Ned and his cousins conducive to work. As he put it in *Something of Myself* –

(Uncle Ned's) golden laugh, his delight in small things, and the perpetual war of practical jokes that waged between us, was refreshment after working hours. And when we cousins, Phil, his son, Stanley Baldwin and I, went to the beach and came back with descriptions of fat bathers, he would draw them indescribably swag-bellied, wallowing in the surf. Those were exceedingly good days, and one's work came easily and fully.

That joy and ease was, sadly, not to last. Uncle Ned died suddenly on 17th June 1898 at his London home, 'The Grange'. His ashes were placed in a corner of St. Margaret's Church to which he had given the three light east window to commemorate his daughter's wedding and which was to receive another two posthumously. Kipling was much saddened by the loss of his uncle, and with cousins and his old Headmaster 'Crom' Price kept vigil over the ashes. When his sister Trix returned from India near the turn of the year she suffered a mental breakdown and had to be cared for at Tisbury, her parents' home. Then in January 1899, at short notice, their plans changed, the family sailed for America to visit Carrie's mother and for Rudyard to attend to some copyright problems. The voyage in a storm-tossed North Atlantic was uncomfortable, but worse was to come. All the family succumbed to feverish illness, Rudyard being stricken with pneumonia which made him delirious. Such was the seriousness that his life was feared for and his condition a matter of concern on both sides of the Atlantic. Tragically, on March 6th, Josephine, the elder daughter died but her father could not be told until he had recovered sufficiently to bear the news. Frank N. Doubleday the publisher; whose 'play-on-initials' produced the nickname 'effendi', and an old friend helped the family during this traumatic time and Rudyard recuperated in New Jersey. The loss of his daughter was a blow from which he never really recovered. Angela Thirkell, Aunt Georgie's grand-daughter wrote in *Three Houses*

Much of the beloved cousin Ruddy of our childhood died with Josephine and I feel that I have never seen him as a real person since that year. There has been the same charm, the same gift of fascinating speech, the same way of making every one with whom he talks show their most interesting side, but one was only allowed to see these things from the other side of a barrier and it was sad for the child who used to be free of the inner courts of his affection.

In June they returned to 'The Elms' but it was more difficult to recapture the spirit which had enabled him, in the first years in Rottingdean, to create with apparently effortless fluency, such stories as *Stalky & Co*, the nursery tales *Just So Stories* and poems like *Our Lady of the Snows* and *The White Man's Burden*. These works had enhanced his already enormous reputation. *Stalky & Co* recalled, with poetic licence, some of the escapades he and his study mates, Stalky, later Major-General L.C. Dunsterville, and M'Turk, C.C. Beresford, got up to whilst at school in Westward Ho!. The *Just So Stories* begun as tales to little children in Vermont and on board ship to South Africa were collected and crafted to become triumphs of 'reading-aloud'. *Our Lady of the Snows* was meant to pay compliment to Canada but it was not looked on with favour in the Dominion because unwittingly his reference to the climate had apparently deterred possible British migrants. *The White Man's Burden* intended as a piece concerned with the responsibilities which colonial powers had towards their territories although welcomed by Theodore Roosevelt offended many in New England. Carrie's diary records the return "The village green is most beautiful. The streets are empty, and we come quietly to The Elms to take on a sort of ghost life. Aunt Georgie meets us at the garden gate." In the weeks that followed, Philip Burne-Jones, who had inherited the Baronetcy created only five years earlier, painted his cousin in the study in 'The Elms', a portrait which was to become one of the best known of all. Kipling said of it, "it's like me at my writing table and as like one pea to another down to the flap of my pocket and the pipe at my side." Another likeness was produced a few months later in South Africa by Mortimer Menpes, showing him in the bush hat and jacket he wore in the Veldt and which was his favourite gear for striding the Downs around Rottingdean.

Rudyard Kipling – the portrait painted by his cousin Philip Burne-Jones is set in the study in 'The Elms' and was done in 1899.

At the beginning of the Boer War in October 1899 Alfred Harmsworth, later Lord Northcliffe, drove down to Rottingdean to ask Kipling to write a poem to help the fund for comforts for the troops overseas and their families. His response produced *The Absent-Minded Beggar* which was to become an immediate best seller and was set to music by Sir Arthur Sullivan who "wedded the words to a tune guaranteed to pull teeth out of barrel-organs." The souvenir edition was published in green script upon cream silk bearing a protrait of the author and a patriotic picture, by Caton Woodville, of a wounded soldier cocking his rifle. The fund achieved enormous success, reaching the staggering sum, for those days, of £250,000. The verses were published first in 'The Daily Mail' on October 31st and Kipling was hard at work on them on the 17th when Henry James came over from Rye to have lunch with the family. The title referred, euphemistically, to the casual way in which the soldiery had always treated the institution of marriage, and was thus particularly appropriate for their dependants, in or out of wedlock. Only a few weeks later the Prime Minister, Lord Salisbury, sent his Private Secretary to 'The Elms' to proffer a knighthood. Carrie noted in her diary "he declined because of his feeling he can do much better work without it. We are much pleased to be offered it however." This was the first refusal of many such non-academic honours.

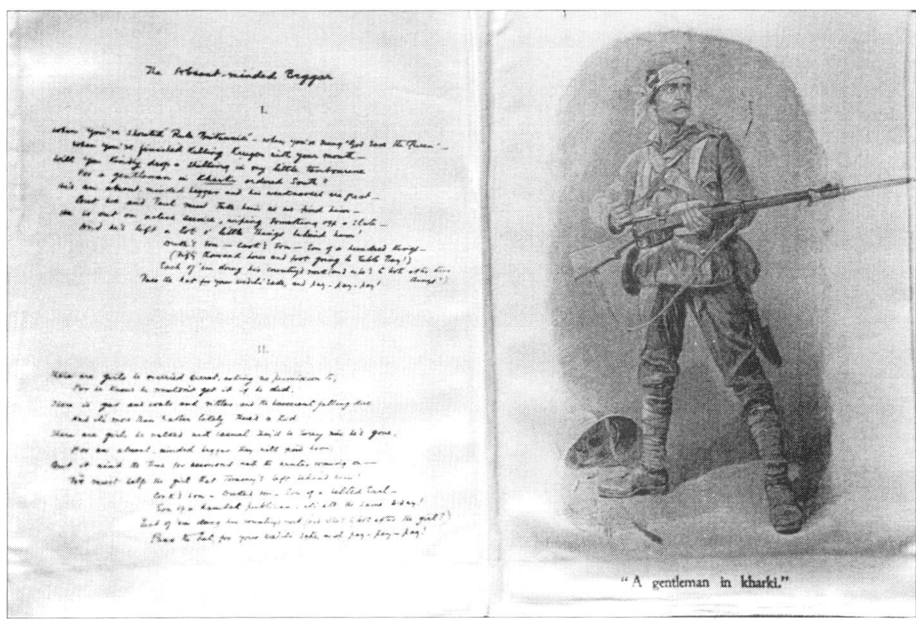

The souvenir edition of 'The Absent-minded beggar' – the inside of the triple folded publication on cream silk. The portrait of the wounded soldier is by Caton-Woodville.

A series of outstanding poems had created the impression in the country that he was, in effect, if not in name, the poet laureate. One of the most popular of the series was *Recessional* written to commemorate the Diamond Jubilee of Queen Victoria two years earlier in 1897. Discarded stanzas of the poem, first entitled 'After', very nearly remained in the waste-paper basket to which they had been consigned. Happily,

Sarah (Sallie) the daughter of an old friend from his American days, C.E. Norton, was staying with the family and, with permission, retrieved the poem. She persuaded Rudyard to seek a second opinion from Aunt Georgie. Their joint approval, having reduced the work from seven stanzas to five, was also instrumental in its despatch, by hand, to Moberly Bell, Manager of 'The Times' who published it on the following day, July 17th. Conflicting accounts have been given as to the precise location of its resurrection – 'The Elms' or 'North End House' – of the manner of its transmission to London, and whether it had been commissioned by Moberly Bell. Publication, later, of a letter which accompanied the poem certainly conveys the impression that no specific commission had been made. *Recessional* became one of his most famous works, although subject to some literary criticism and disapproval by those who seemed determined to misinterpret the sentiments expressed. It was started on Jubilee Day, June 22nd 1897 when he set aside other work to crystallise his ideas to commemorate the celebration. The weather was dull and overcast but began to brighten towards evening when he and Carrie went out to listen to the peal of bells from St. Margaret's and to watch a bonfire on Beacon Hill, one of a chain lit to mark the special day . . This seems to find expression in the third stanza – *On dune and headland sinks the fire; Lo all our pomp of yesterday Is one with Ninevah and Tyre.* Almost immediately after the Jubilee he went off to H.M.S. Pelorus as guest of Captain Bagley, for the Naval Review and subsequent manoeuvres. Some weeks elapsed before, with Sallie's initiative, the poem was retrieved and completed. The poem's title, the hymn sung whilst choir and clergy retire at the end of a service, is incorporated in the name of a chapel, modelled exactly upon St. Margaret's, built in Forest Lawn Memorial Park in Glendale, California, where it is 'The Church of the Recessional'.

Shortly after the welcome reception of *Recessional* an even more satisfying event took place. On August 17th their first and only son was born at 'North End House'. In a letter to W.J. Harding, Kipling is clearly still enthusiastic about nautical matters, for he writes amusingly:-

Ref: t.b.d. trials. My attention is at present taken up by one small craft recently launched from my own works – weight (approx) 8.957 lbs: h.p. (indicated) 2.0464, consumption of fuel unrecorded but fresh supplies needed every 2 ½ hrs. The vessel at present needs at least 15 years for full completion but at the end of that time may be an efficient addition to the Navy, for which service it is intended. Date of launch Aug.17th 1.50 a.m. No casualties. Christened John. You will understand that the new craft requires a certain amount of attention – but I trust ere long to be able to attend a t.b.d. trial.

Kipling had presumably been invited to another sea-going exercise in a torpedo-boat destroyer. John's earliest years were spent at 'The Elms' and in a private letter to Dora Clarke (later Lady Mansergh) on the birth of her daughter Hilary, his God-daughter, Kipling recalls "When my boy was born I wheeled the pram up and down across Rottingdene green – and was rather proud of it." Even after the move to 'Bateman's', John maintained contact with the village for he was at Preparatory School, St. Aubyn's, and was thus able to visit his Aunt just up the road. Hopes for his son's entry to the Royal Navy never materialised for John's poor eyesight precluded acceptance. John was to attempt to join the army on his seventeenth birthday in 1914 but again his eyesight proved a barrier. An approach to an old friend of his father, Lord Roberts, enabled him to join the Irish Guards the following month. Two days before his next birthday John left for the Front and, with so many other sons, was reported missing during the Battle of Loos on October 2nd. For long his parents nursed the hope that he might be a prisoner of war, until eventually they had to accept the inevitable.

The early part of the Kiplings' time in Rottingdean was, as already noted, particularly happy. The children, with their father and his cousins were able to enjoy the beach and fish from the pier recently installed to receive the 'Brighton and Rottingdean Seashore Electric Railway' alias 'Daddy-Long-Legs', a remarkable construction of the ever inventive Magnus Volk. Kipling delighted in the children's play, acting with and reading to Josephine, Elsie and Angela Mackail who were obviously enthralled by the lack of condescension usually shown by adults. This ability to enter whole-heartedly into the world of children was apparent wherever he encountered them, as so often on the long sea voyages to South Africa. It was perhaps this gift which made him so marvellous a writer of stories for the young. He also delighted in visits from his parents, Lockwood and Alice from their Wiltshire home, from other relations and from his old Headmaster, Cormell Price, known as 'Uncle Crom', for whom he had a great affection and who had first encouraged the bespectacled 'Gigger' in literary appreciation and in writing for the school magazine. Kipling's nickname 'Gigger' came from the thick lenses he had to wear and which reminded his school chums of the lamps of a gig, a two-wheeled pony and trap.

The Rottingdean terminus of the Brighton and Rottingdean Seashore Electric Railway, known as 'Daddy-Long-Legs'. One of Magnus Volk's inventions, it ran from Paston Place, Brighton between 1896 and 1901 until the rails attached to concrete blocks on the foreshore were too badly storm-damaged.

He also found time to organise local volunteers in preparation for the war which, with the prescience of other great men, he felt inevitably threatened from across the channel. In 1900 he founded a Rifle Club, using a miniature range in the tin Drill Hall on the site of what is now the Convent, and a full 900 yard range across Lustrells, towards the steep slopes of Telscombe Tye. His assistants as instructors were an ex-service man, Mr J.S. Johnson, employed as the Sergeant Instructor at Rottingdean School, one of the local prep-schools and Petty Officers of the Coastguard. He prepared full instructions for the continuity of training whilst he was away in South Africa. His belief in Empire and his patriotism were thus not mere expressions of hope but were translated into really practical opportunities, albeit on a small scale. Later he wrote extensively about Naval and Army training, but this volunteer form of service perhaps crystallised the ideas which were shortly turned to prose in the two part *The Army of a Dream*. Here he envisages a somewhat far-fetched notion of the population of Britain united in a service which, whilst incorporating a certain degree of social engineering, created a force which would stand against all possible attacks. The same sort of theme was restated in a poem *The Islanders* in which he makes a plea for the nation to take the defence of the realm as seriously as many of its citizens took organized games. The oft-quoted lines *With the flannelled fools at the wicket or the muddied oafs at the goals* caused considerable resentment to those throughout the social spectrum. Again he was misunderstood for he suggested later in a letter to his great friend Rider Haggard that he should have used the word 'hired' in place of 'flannelled'. He was commenting on the absurdity of professional cricket in wartime. England was winning a three day match in Australia as the poem was published. He, with 'The Times' recognised the disproportionate importance given in the newspapers to a game of cricket.

It is possible too, that whilst in Rottingdean his thoughts turned to smuggling. With village traditions, the maze of underground tunnels and the former Customs House, 'Tallboys' it could scarcely fail to do so. It was well known that a former Vicar, the Rev. Dr. Hooker, had acted as look-out man for the smugglers way back in the last decade of the Eighteenth Century. Kipling later used a smuggling tale in *Puck of Pook's Hill* and wrote one of his most evocative poems *A Smugglers' Song* in which a mother tells her child to *Watch the wall, my darling, while the Gentlemen go by.*

Later on the time spent in Rottingdean was less idyllic mainly because of the tragic loss of Josephine in New York in March 1899. He and Carrie could not forget the happy times and were constantly imagining that they saw their precious first-born in the house and garden. The familiar scenes began to haunt them. He expressed his intense sorrow in a poem called *Merrow Down* which he wrote whilst on a visit to his father's old friends, the St. Loe Strachey's, near Guildford some two years later. The loss also seemed to find expression in the short story *They* in *Traffics and Discoveries*. Here he describes the Sussex Countryside, explored when house hunting in the area around Washington, where in a strange mansion he encounters the blind woman and her dream children. This unassuaged sadness, together with growing local frustrations and ideological conflict led them to seek the sanctuary which eventually came with the move to 'Batemans'.

His was a restless mind, always seeking new strands to commit to memory and then to paper. Each winter he spent abroad, in South Africa, or as in the devastating early months of 1899 in the United States. He rejoiced in being able, in South Africa, to renew his press work for the soldier's newspaper, the Bloemfontein 'Friend', and came under fire whilst reporting the Battle of Kari Siding. He was able to talk with, and perhaps influence, some of the greatest characters on the world stage – Cecil Rhodes, Dr Jameson and Lord Milner. Jameson's strength of personality was later adopted for the exceptionally popular poem *If.* By a strange coincidence a later occupant of 'North End House' and an owner of 'The Elms', Sir Roderick Jones, also came within Dr Jameson's ambit whilst in South Africa during his early days with Reuter's, the firm he was eventually to direct. Back in England Kipling was still restless, enjoying the early and often frustrating pleasures of motoring. He developed an empathy with all mechanical contrivances, although it was usually other folks who got their fingers oily. He loved his excursions with the Fleet to which he was invited by a succession of Captains, and these adventures inspired some naval stories. They also evoked some humorous private correspondence, as in the piece to Captain Norbury on board H.M.S. Pelorus in which he cleverly introduced the name of every ship in the squadron. In July 1901 he was guest of Commander H.J.L. Clarke in H.M.S. Nile. On his return he sent a gift to the Wardroom accompanied by a letter:-

To President W R NILE
Dear Sir,
I have the honour to forward herewith for information and reference one (1) complete set of the prose works of Mr. Rudyard Kipling an author for whom (Though I never yet had the pleasure of meeting him) I entertain a sincere regard. You will find his works elevating Innocuous and strictly moral. Some of his sentences are beautiful while others are even more so & the refinement of his language is only equalled by the aristocratic interests of his characters.

If the perusal of his pure and lofty style should in any way tend to the amelioration of the manners and customs of the King's Navy a service which I understand is composed exclusively of large hairy men without boots I shall feel that Mr. Kipling's labours have not been in vain.

Vy sincerely yours
Rud K

PS The bulk of the works have gone down direct from London. The volume that accompanies this is a little tract upon Life in the Army & is distinguished by a chastity of diction & a pungent lucidity of intellect which has seldom been equalled.

The recipient, his friend, Commander Clarke was later to become a resident of the village when he bought 'Hillside' from Ernest Beard in 1911.

Although the Kiplings' first contact with Bateman's and the spell it was to weave about them came to naught, they persisted in their house hunting, doing considerable mileage in a succession of cars including a 'steamer'. He had caught the infection of motoring on the day back in 1899 when Alfred Harmsworth came to 'The Elms' about help for the South African Fund and also demonstrated his new horseless carriage. Fortunately Bateman's came back on to the market and they recognised immediately that the Spirit of the House – her Feng Shui – was benevolent. Shortly after the end of the Boer War the purchase was completed and in the first week of September 1902 they moved from the Rottingdean which held such bitter-sweet memories. They would no longer be plagued by trippers wishing to catch a glimpse of the great man at work in his study window, or as in one instance, recorded by Angela Thirkell, of a young lady asking to be directed to where she understood the poet to be buried. No longer would the throng at the gates be parted to allow Carrie through, nor would the redoubtable Mrs Ridsdale parry enquiries as to his whereabouts with "What have you read of his?". An unsatisfactory answer would elicit the response "Then I won't tell you!"

Detail from a longer photograph of skating on the village pond at the turn of the Century. 'The Elms' is behind the two foreground figures and 'Northgate House' looms faintly on the horizon.

Thankfully, although the village has grown out of all Kipling's recognition, the Green and the Garden, so imaginatively restored by the Rottingdean Preservation Society, still convey an impression of the tranquillity which, trippers apart, he and the family so much appreciated. Although written later, the poem *The Glory of the Garden* is perfect for the setting of The Kipling Garden and he would have appreciated the appropriateness of his words to the present landscaping of the enclosed plot he once enjoyed. 'The Elms' stands more exposed than it did at the turn of the century when there were more trees within the walled island.

Other writers have had close connection with the village. Angela Thirkell has already been mentioned and Enid Bagnold, the wife of Sir Roderick Jones, a subsequent owner of 'North End House' set the early chapters of 'National Velvet' and her play 'The Chalk Garden' here. William Black, a popular Victorian novelist, was a local resident. But Rudyard Kipling was unquestionably the greatest, and though Rottingdean is fortunate to be able to claim part of him, but he was equally fortunate to know and to love the village and its unspoiled encircling Downland and shore.

THE POEMS

The poems which are printed in full are some of those most especially connected with Rottingdean, either because they relate to the surrounding Downland scenery or because they were written during the Rottingdean years. T.S. Eliot once wrote that Kipling had "a consummate gift of word, phrase, and rhythm" and suggested that he was a great writer of verse rather than poetry. The latter remark is perhaps intended for the specialist but to most of us the variety of form, the range of topics and the use of a number of dialects delight the ear and make us think that this is a poetry we can understand and appreciate. Many of his poems are best read aloud and even though we may not be able to 'do' a regional burr for *Sussex* or *A Smugglers' Song* or the Cockney called for in *An Absent-Minded Beggar* it is fun to try. Reading aloud can almost be so soft that only the speaker hears it. Kipling would have appreciated the thought of many still unborn mouthing the stanzas he penned. The poems are a mirror to his times but they are also there to be enjoyed. Their enjoyment may lead to a wider and deeper acquaintance with his vast output on countless topics.

RECESSIONAL

God of our fathers, known of old,
Lord of our far-flung battle-line,
Beneath whose awful Hand we hold
Dominion over palm and pine –
Lord God of Hosts, be with us yet,
Lest we forget – lest we forget!

The tumult and the shouting dies;
The Captains and the Kings depart:
Still stands thy ancient sacrifice,
An humble and a contrite heart.
Lord God of Hosts, be with us yet,
Lest we forget – lest we forget!

continued ...

Far-called, our navies melt away;
On dune and headland sinks the fire:
Lo, all our pomp of yesterday
Is one with Ninevah and Tyre!
Judge of the Nations, spare us yet,
Lest we forget – lest we forget!

If, drunk with sight of power, we loose
Wild tongues that have not Thee in awe,
Such boastings as the Gentiles use,
Or lesser breeds without the Law –
Lord God of Hosts, be with us yet,
Lest we forget – lest we forget!

For heathen heart that puts her trust
In reeking tube and iron shard,
All valiant dust that builds on dust,
And guarding, calls not Thee to guard,
For frantic boast and foolish word –
Thy mercy on Thy People, Lord!

The poem written to celebrate the sixtieth anniversary of Queen Victoria's reign received enormous acclaim. Although misinterpreted by some, perhaps deliberately, it stressed the need for those controlling affairs of state to be filled with humility, with reverence, and with a regard for 'the Law'. It attracted some criticism from those who felt that he had based it, whether in metre or in phrase, on the work of others. This, surely, is wholly unworthy and unwarranted. The praise from friends and colleagues was treasured by the Kipling family because it suggested that he had, once more, correctly assessed the mood of the nation at the time. It was set to music as a hymn by Sir Arthur Sullivan and became a firm favourite.

THE ABSENT-MINDED BEGGAR

When you've shouted "Rule Britannia", when you've sung "God Save the Queen",
When you've finished killing Kruger with your mouth,
Will you kindly drop a shilling in my little tambourine
For a gentleman in khaki ordered South?
He's an absent-minded beggar, and his weaknesses are great –
But we and Paul must take him as we find him –
He's out on active service, wiping something off a slate –
And he's left a lot of little things behind him!
Duke's son – cook's son – son of a hundred kings –
(Fifty thousand horse and foot going to Table Bay!)

continued . . .

Each of 'em doing his country's work
(and who's to look after their things?)
Pass the hat for your credit's sake,
and pay – pay – pay!

There are girls he married secret, asking no permission to,
For he knew he wouldn't get it if he did.
There is gas and coal and vittles, and the house-rent falling due,
And it's more than rather likely there's a kid.
There are girls he walked with casual. They'll be sorry now he's gone,
For an absent-minded beggar they will find him,
But it ain't the time for sermons with the winter coming on.
We must help the girl that Tommy's left behind him!
Cook's son – Duke's son – son of a belted Earl –
Son of a Lambeth publican – it's all the same today!
Each of 'em doing his country's work
(and who's to look after the girl?)
Pass the hat for your credit's sake,
and pay – pay – pay!

There are families by thousands, far too proud to beg or speak,
And they'll put their sticks and bedding up the spout,
And they'll live on half o' nothing, paid 'em punctual once a week,
'Cause the man that earns the wage is ordered out.
He's an absent-minded beggar, but he heard his country call,
And his reg'ment didn't need to send to find him!
He chucked his job and joined it – so the job before us all
Is to help the home that Tommy's left behind him!
Duke's job – cook's job – gardener, baronet, groom,
Mews or palace or paper-shop, there's someone gone away!
Each of 'em doing his country's work
(And who's to look after the room?)
Pass the hat for your credit's sake,
and pay – pay – pay!

Let us manage so as, later, we can look him in the face,
And tell him what he'd very much prefer –
That while he saved the Empire, his employer saved his place,
And his mates (that's you and me) looked out for her.
He's an absent-minded beggar and he may forget it all,
But we do not want his kiddies to remind him
That we sent 'em to the workhouse while their daddy hammered Paul,
So we'll help the homes that Tommy left behind him!

continued . . .

Cook's home – Duke's home – home of a millionaire,
(Fifty thousand horse and foot going to Table Bay!)
Each of 'em doing his country's work
(and what have you got to spare?)
Pass the hat for your credit's sake,
and pay – pay – pay!

Paul Kruger was the President of the Transvaal at the head of the movement to free Dutch South Africa from all British control. In October 1899 the Boers invaded Natal and Cape Colony in order, they claimed, to anticipate a threatened attack by the British. Britain was poorly equipped to deal with the situation and the Imperial force in Natal under Sir George White, badly outnumbered, was soon beseiged in Ladysmith. Meanwhile at Mafeking, Lieutenant-Colonel Baden-Powell was surrounded in the small trading station whose defence was to become legend.

An army was sent from England commanded by Sir Redvers Buller. This was split on arrival to attempt to raise the various seiges. One group under Buller, making its way to relieve Ladysmith, was checked and soundly defeated. His skill as a commander was increasingly called into question. It became clear that reinforcements were needed and more than 200,000 troops were sent to South Africa. Many militia, volunteers and yeomanry responded to the call, as well as contingents from other Dominions. This force was commanded by Lord Roberts who replaced Buller as C-in-C and his skill enabled him to lift the siege of Kimberley and take Bloemfontein, whilst at the same time Buller eventually relieved Ladysmith. The Mafeking Relief Force was able to raise the seige of 217 days, an event which caused widespread rejoicing back home because the courage and resourcefulness of Baden-Powell and his garrison had captured the imagination of the British people. On June 5th Roberts took Pretoria, the capital of the Transvaal, Kruger, however, escaping into exile. These successes seemed decisive and Roberts returned home in November 1900. His successor, Kitchener, was faced with a different kind of war which dragged on for another eighteen months. British troops were continually harrassed by the Boer commandos, whose guerilla tactics were unfamiliar and difficult to combat. Superior mobility, excellent marksmanship and local knowledge ensured that the conflict was protracted even against so large a force. After a harrowing campaign in which the civilian population suffered badly, the Boers were finally forced to sue for peace at the Treaty of Vereeniging on 31st May 1902.

SUSSEX

God gave all men all earth to love,
But, since our hearts are small,
Ordained for each one spot should prove
Belovèd over all;
That, as He watched Creation's birth,
So we, in godlike mood,
May of our love create our earth
And see that it is good.

So one shall Baltic pines content,
As one some Surrey glade,
Or one the palm-grove's droned lament
Before Levuka's Trade.
Each to his choice, and I rejoice
The lot has fallen to me
In a fair ground – in a fair ground –
Yea, Sussex by the sea!

No tender-hearted garden crowns,
No bosomed woods adorn
Our blunt, bow-headed, whale-backed Downs,
But gnarled and writhen thorn –
Bare slopes where chasing shadows skim,
And, through the gaps revealed,
Belt upon belt, the wooded, dim,
Blue goodness of the Weald.

Clean of officious fence or hedge,
Half-wild and wholly tame,
The wise turf cloaks the white cliff-edge
As when the Romans came.
What sign of those that fought and died
At shift of sword and sword?
The barrow and the camp abide,
The sunlight and the sward.

Here leaps ashore the full Sou'west
All heavy-winged with brine,
Here lies above the folded crest
The Channel's leaden line;
And here the sea-fogs lap and cling,
And here, each warning each,
The sheep-bells and the ship-bells ring
Along the hidden beach.

We have no waters to delight
Our broad and brookless vales –
Only the dewpond on the height
Unfed, that never fails –
Whereby no tattered herbage tells
Which way the season flies –
Only our close-bit thyme that smells
Like dawn in Paradise.

Here through the strong and shadeless days
The tinkling silence thrills;
Or little, lost, Down churches praise
The Lord who made the hills:
But here the Old Gods guard their round,
And, in her secret heart,
The heathen kingdom Wilfrid found
Dreams, as she dwells, apart.

Though all the rest were all my share,
With equal soul I'd see
Her nine-and-thirty sisters fair,
Yet none more fair than she.
Choose ye your need from Thames to Tweed,
And I will choose instead
Such lands as lie 'twixt Rake and Rye,
Black Down and Beachy Head.

I will go out against the sun
Where the rolled scarp retires,
And the Long Man of Wilmington
Looks naked toward the shires;
And east till doubling Rother crawls
To find the fickle tide,
By dry and sea-forgotten walls,
Our ports of stranded pride.

I will go north about the shaws
And the deep ghylls that breed
Huge oaks and old, the which we hold
No more than Sussex weed;
Or south where windy Piddinghoe's
Begilded dolphin veers,
And red beside wide-bankèd Ouse
Lie down our Sussex steers.

So to the land our hearts we give
Till the sure magic strike,
And Memory, Use and Love make live
Us and our fields alike –
That deeper than our speech and thought,
Beyond our reason's sway,
Clay of the pit whence we were wrought
Yearns to its fellow-clay.

God gives all men all earth to love,
But, since man's heart is small,
Ordains for each one spot shall prove
Belovèd over all.
Each to his choice, and I rejoice
The lot has fallen to me
In a fair ground – in a fair ground –
Yea, Sussex by the sea!

Sussex illustrates Kipling's extraordinary capacity to get right to the heart of his subject and then to paint a word picture which evokes, exactly, its mood and nature. *Ordained for each one spot should prove Beloved over all"* is fittingly inscribed onto the stone seat at The Devil's Dyke, near Brighton. The great descriptive phrases begin in the third stanza. The traditional Downland landscape whose rounded contours are coated in a short springy turf are *Our blunt, bow-headed, whale-backed Downs* and later he recognises the essentially arid nature of the chalk with *We have no waters to delight Our broad and brookless vales* and the cropped turf with *Only our close-bit thyme that smells Like dawn in Paradise.* The dew-ponds, made during the past two centuries, provided the great sheep flocks with water, although those flocks were the basis for the Downland economy many centuries before. His familiarity with the distinctive landforms of the swelling Downs came as a result of the walks he made during his Rottingdean years.

The coastline is equally appreciated with *The wise turf cloaks the white cliff edge* and the way in which some of the lowland coasts have advanced with the deposition of sand and shingle to leave *Our ports of stranded pride* – particularly, but not exclusively, Rye and Winchelsea. Neither does he ignore the contrasting landscape of *the wooded, dim, Blue goodness of the Weald* to which he was shortly to move. He refers to the 'shaws', the relic woodland, and the 'deep ghylls' which cut into the flanks of the high plateau of Ashdown Forest. The imprint of man is suggested by the reference to The Long Man of Wilmington, the great chalk line drawing cradled in his coombe on Wind'oer Hill, and the belated conversion of the heathen Saxon by Wilfrid, an exiled Northumbrian bishop. A certain amount of poetic licence has transformed the salmon-trout weather vane of St John's Church at Piddinghoe into a "Beguilded dolphin".

Sussex by the sea could not have been given a more evocative eulogy!

THE RUN OF THE DOWNS

The Weald is good, the Downs are best –
I'll give you the run of 'em, East to West.
Beachy Head and Winddoor Hill,
They were once and they are still.
Firle, Mount Caburn and Mount Harry
Go back as far as sums'll carry.
Ditchling Beacon and Chanctonbury Ring,
They have looked on many a thing;
And what those two have missed between 'em
I reckon Truleigh Hill has seen 'em.
Highden, Bignor and Duncton Down
Knew Old England before the Crown.
Linch Down, Treyford and Sunwood
Knew Old England before the Flood.
And when you end on the Hampshire side –
Butser's old as Time and Tide.
The Downs are sheep, the Weald is corn,
You be glad you are Sussex born!

This little piece is reminiscent of the old 'capes and bays' geography of the kind taught when Kipling was in the classroom, when pupils had to learn by rote the names of towns or landscape features in sequence. But it is more than that, for it poses the age old distinction in Sussex between the rival claims of the bold, often bare outlines of the chalk Downs and the contrasting landscapes of the sandstone plateau of the High Weald and the broad clay vale of the Low weald. Here he extols the chalk, but the contrasting claims are more fully explored in *The Knife and the Naked Chalk.*

The poem will certainly appeal to keen walkers of the South Downs Way to whom it will read like a succession of signposts.

A SMUGGLERS' SONG

If you wake at midnight, and hear a horse's feet,
Don't go drawing back the blind, or looking in the street,
Them that asks no questions isn't told a lie.
Watch the wall, my darling, while the Gentlemen go by!
Five-and-twenty ponies,
Trotting through the dark –
Brandy for the Parson,
'Baccy for the Clerk;
Laces for a lady; letters for a spy,
And watch the wall, my darling, while the Gentlemen go by!

continued . . .

Running round the woodlump if you chance to find
Little barrels, roped and tarred, all full of brandy-wine;
Don't you shout to come and look, nor take 'em for your play;
Put the brishwood back again, – and they'll be gone next day!

If you see the stable-door setting open wide;
If you see a tired horse lying down inside;
If your mother mends a coat cut about and tore;
If the lining's wet and warm – don't you ask no more!

If you meet King George's men, dressed in blue and red,
You be careful what you say, and mindful what is said.
If they call you 'pretty maid', and chuck you 'neath the chin,
Don't you tell where no one is, nor yet where no one's been!

Knocks and footsteps round the house – whistles after dark –
You've no call for running out till the house-dogs bark.
Trusty's here, and Pincher's here, and see how dumb they lie –
They don't fret to follow when the Gentlemen go by!

If you do as you've been told, likely there's a chance
You'll be give a dainty doll, all the way from France,
With a cap of Valenciennes, and a velvet hood –
A present from the Gentlemen, along o' being good!
Five-and-twenty ponies,
Trotting through the dark –
Brandy for the Parson,
'Baccy for the Clerk.
Them that asks no questions isn't told a lie –
Watch the wall, my darling, while the Gentlemen go by!

Whilst the germ of this smuggling poem may well have been born in Rottingdean, a community still trading on the soubriquet "smugglers' village" the most familiar line *Watch the wall, my darling, while the gentlemen go by* was almost certainly one he heard from a Burwash woman. Both places were closely connected with the movement of contraband, the whole of the Sussex coast providing suitable dropping points which fed inland tracks leading to the lucrative London market. *Brandy for the parson* was a commonplace and in Rottingdean, the Vicar of a century before, the Rev. Dr. Hooker, was usually cited as an example of one of the cloth in league with the 'honest thieves'. There was still a residual presence of the Coastguard at Saltdean when Kipling was in residence and some of the officers assisted him with the organisation of the Rifle Club. The presence of many substantial passages and tunnels beneath houses right up to the Green gave credence to the sorts of tales which would have abounded.

THE GLORY OF THE GARDEN

Our England is a garden that is full of stately views,
Of borders, beds and shrubberies and lawns and avenues,
With statues on the terraces and peacocks strutting by;
But the Glory of the Garden lies in more than meets the eye.

For where the old thick laurels grow, along the thin red wall,
You'll find the tool- and potting-sheds which are the heart of all;
The cold-frames and the hot-houses, the dung-pits and the tanks,
The rollers, carts and drain-pipes, with the barrows and the planks.

And there you'll see the gardeners, the men and 'prentice boys,
Told off to do what they are bid and do it without noise;
For, except when seeds are planted and we shout to scare the birds,
The Glory of the Garden it abideth not in words.

And some can pot begonias and some can bud a rose,
And some are hardly fit to trust with anything that grows;
But they can roll and trim the lawns and sift the sand and loam,
For the Glory of the Garden occupieth all who come.

Our England is a garden, and such gardens are not made
By singing:- "Oh, how beautiful!" and sitting in the shade,
While better men than we go out and start their working lives
At grubbing weeds from gravel-paths with broken dinner-knives.

There's not a pair of legs so thin, there's not a head so thick,
There's not a hand so weak and white, nor yet a heart so sick,
But it can find some needful job that's crying to be done,
For the Glory of the Garden glorifieth every one.

Then seek your job with thankfulness and work till further orders,
If it's only netting strawberries or killing slugs on borders;
And when your back stops aching and your hands begin to harden,
You will find yourself a partner in the Glory of the Garden.

Oh, Adam was a gardener, and God who made him sees
That half a proper gardener's work is done upon his knees,
So when your work is finished, you can wash your hands and pray
For the Glory of the Garden, that it may not pass away!
And the Glory of the garden it shall never pass away!

Nothing could be more appropriate for the Kipling Garden in Rottingdean than these verses, written in 1910 for C.R.L. Fletcher's *History of England*. Although it doesn't cover the acreage of the gardens of a great stately home and doesn't have all the sheds and work spaces one used to find there, it epitomises what Kipling had to say. He would surely have approved and applauded what the Rottingdean Preservation Society has done, first to ensure that this little plot was not lost to more bricks and mortar and then to transform an overgrown wilderness into an oasis of calm and beauty and fragrance for all to enjoy for ever.

CHRONOLOGY OF THE ROTTINGDEAN YEARS

1882	First visit 'en-route' to India to stay with Aunt Georgie at 'North End House'
1897 June	Moved in with the Burne-Jones at 'North End House', working on *The White Man's Burden*
	Fleet manoeuvres from Portsmouth in HMS Pelorus
July 17	*Recessional* published in The Times
Aug 17	Birth of John
	Family in residence at 'The Elms'
1898 Jan 8	Sailed for South Africa
Jan 25	to Newlands – Lockwood with them – met Cecil Rhodes
	Kipling to Kimberley, Bulawayo, Johannesburg
April	back home
	working on *Kim* & *Stalky*
June 17	Death of 'Uncle Ned' (Sir Edward Burne-Jones)
Sept	with HMS Pelorus in Irish Sea
	The Days Work published
1899 Jan 25	sailed for U.S.A. to see Carrie's parents
Feb 2	Docked in New York
4	*The White Man's Burden* published in 'The Times'
5	Joesphine taken ill
21	Rudyard Kipling ill
Mar 6	Josephine dies but Kipling too ill to be told
April 17	Convalescence in Lakewood, New Jersey
May	Morristown
June 24	Return to 'The Elms'
July	Portrait by Philip Burne-Jones
Aug	Sutherland – fishing
	back in Rottingdean
	work with Volunteers
Oct 6	*Stalky & Co* published
Oct 11	Government declares war on Boers
	Visit of Alfred Harmsworth re verse for South Africa fund
Oct 31	*The Absent-Minded Beggar* published in Daily Mail
Dec 14	Offer of Knighthood – declined
1900 Jan 20	Sailed for South Africa
Feb 5	stayed at Mount Nelson Hotel
Mar	helped edit 'The Friend' a paper for the troops
Mar 29	Battle of Kari Siding
Apr 3	Back at Capetown
May 18	return to Rottingdean
	news of Relief of Mafeking – cannon fired to welcome men home – general jubilation – except by Aunt Georgie, Margaret and Jack Mackail
July	organising Rottingdean Rifle Club – range in Lustrells and a miniature one in tin drill shed on site of the Convent
Aug	House hunting – by train to Etchingham and 'fly' to Batemans. Their hesitation lost it for the time being
Dec	worked on *The Army of a Dream* during voyage south
Dec 25	return to South Africa – to 'The Woolsack' on the 'Groote Schuur' estate built for them by Cecil Rhodes.
1901	Publication of *Kim*
Feb	Plans with Rhodes for 'Rhodes Scholarships'
Apr	Back in Rottingdean
June	Visit to Paris with American friends
July	to Tisbury to his parents and then to HMS Nile as guest of Commander H.J.L. Clarke
Aug	*The Islanders* – poetic plea to take national service as seriously as games like cricket and football

continued . . .

1902 Jan	To the Cape again
Mar 26	Death of Cecil Rhodes
Apr 3	Kipling reads his verses *The Burial* at the State funeral
	He completes the poem *Sussex*
	Return to Rottingdean
	His mother and sister stay at 'The Elms'
May 31	Boer War ends with the Treaty of Vereeniging
June 1	rejoicing in Rottingdean except by Aunt Georgie who displays banner. Rudyard Kipling and 'Ambo' Poynter pacify crowd
10	'Bateman's' purchased
Sept 2	Caroline effects move
3	Rudyard Kipling moves in

REFERENCES

by Rudyard Kipling:-

PROSE

AUTOBIOGRAPHY –

Something of Myself — Macmillan 1937

FICTION

Stalky & Co — Macmillan 1899

Kim — Macmillan 1901

Just-So Stories — Macmillan 1902

The Knife and the Naked Chalk (Rewards & Fairies) — Macmillan 1910

They (Traffics & Discoveries) — Macmillan 1904

The Army of a Dream (Traffics & Discoveries) — 1904

POETRY

Our Lady of the Snows — 1897

Recessional — 1897

The White Man's Burden — 1899

The Absent-Minded Beggar — 1899

Merrow Down (Just-So Stories) — 1902

The Islanders — 1901

The Burial — 1902

Sussex (The Five Nations) — 1903

A Smugglers' Song (Puck of Pook's Hill) — 1906

The Glory of the Garden (with C.R.L. Fletcher; A History of England) — 1910

The Run of the Downs (Rewards and Fairies) — 1910

If (Rewards & Fairies) — 1910

MAJOR BIOGRAPHIES

Birkenhead, Lord *Rudyard Kipling* — Weidenfeld & Nicholson 1978

Carrington C. *Rudyard Kipling – His Life & Work* — Macmillan 1955

Fido M. *Rudyard Kipling – An Illustrated Biography* — Hamlyn 1974

Laski M. *From Palm to Pine – Rudyard Kipling Abroad and at Home* — Sidgwick & Jackson 1987

Thurston Hopkins R. *Rudyard Kipling – The Story of a Genius* — Palmer 1930

Wilson A. *The Strange Ride of Rudyard Kipling* — Secker & Warburg 1977

OTHER WORKS

Cohen M. (Ed) *Rudyard Kipling to Rider Haggard* — Hutchinson 1965

Copper, Bob *A Song for Every Season* — Heinemann 1971

Copper, Bob *Early to Rise* — Heinemann 1976

Moens S.M. *Rottingdean – The Story of a Village* — Beal 1953

Thirkell A. *Three Houses* — O.U.P. 1931

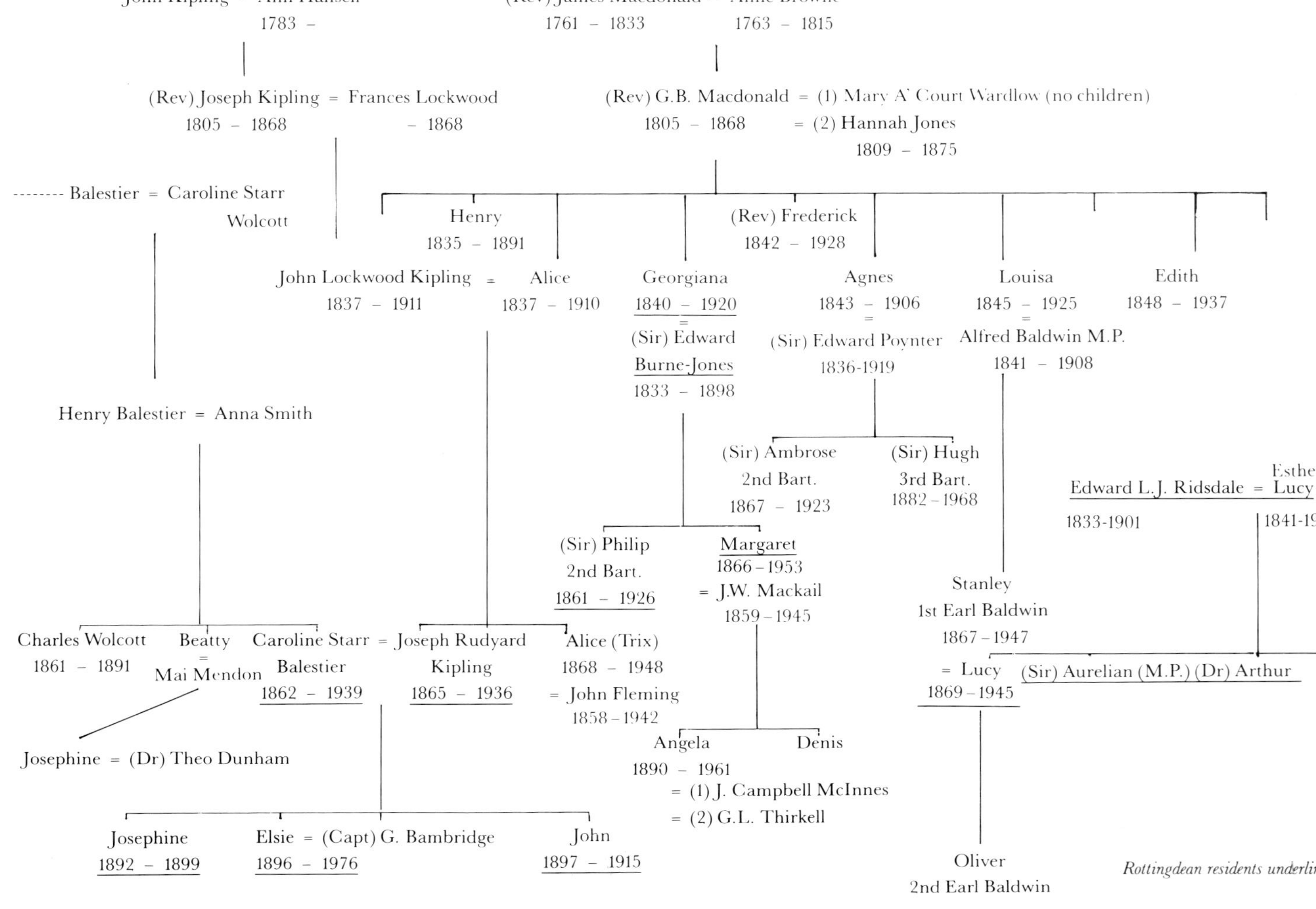
John Kipling = Ann Hansell
1783 –
(Rev) James Macdonald = Anne Browne
1761 – 1833
1763 – 1815
(Rev) Joseph Kipling = Frances Lockwood
1805 – 1868
– 1868
(Rev) G.B. Macdonald = (1) Mary A' Court Wardlow (no children)
1805 – 1868
= (2) Hannah Jones
1809 – 1875
-------- Balestier = Caroline Starr Wolcott
Henry
1835 – 1891
(Rev) Frederick
1842 – 1928
John Lockwood Kipling = Alice
1837 – 1911
1837 – 1910
Georgiana
1840 – 1920
= (Sir) Edward Burne-Jones
1833 – 1898
Agnes
1843 – 1906
= (Sir) Edward Poynter
1836-1919
Louisa
1845 – 1925
= Alfred Baldwin M.P.
1841 – 1908
Edith
1848 – 1937
Henry Balestier = Anna Smith
(Sir) Ambrose
2nd Bart.
1867 – 1923
(Sir) Hugh
3rd Bart.
1882 – 1968
Edward L.J. Ridsdale = Esther Lucy
1833-1901
1841-1901
(Sir) Philip
2nd Bart.
1861 – 1926
Margaret
1866 – 1953
= J.W. Mackail
1859 – 1945
Stanley
1st Earl Baldwin
1867 – 1947
Charles Wolcott
1861 – 1891
Beatty
= Mai Mendon
Caroline Starr Balestier
1862 – 1939
= Joseph Rudyard Kipling
1865 – 1936
Alice (Trix)
1868 – 1948
= John Fleming
1858 – 1942
= Lucy
1869 – 1945
(Sir) Aurelian (M.P.)
(Dr) Arthur
Lily
Josephine = (Dr) Theo Dunham
Angela
1890 – 1961
= (1) J. Campbell McInnes
= (2) G.L. Thirkell
Denis
Josephine
1892 – 1899
Elsie = (Capt) G. Bambridge
1896 – 1976
John
1897 – 1915
Oliver
2nd Earl Baldwin
Rottingdean residents underlined